NICK BUTTERWORTH AND MICK INKPEN

THE HOUSE ON THE ROCK

CANDLE
BOOKS

To help people understand what God is like,
Jesus told lots of stories which are as exciting
today as when they were first heard.

The House On The Rock is still a great favourite
and its message is one that children especially
love to hear.

Text and illustrations copyright © 1986, 1989 Nick Butterworth and Mick Inkpen.
First published by Marshall, Morgan & Scott.

Published by Candle Books
an imprint of
Lion Hudson plc
Wilkinson House, Jordan Hill Road,
Oxford OX2 8DR, England
www.lionhudson.com/candle

ISBN 978 1 85985 749 6

First edition 2008

International publishing rights owned by Zondervan®.

Acknowledgments
Scripture quotations in this book are taken from the Good News Bible © 1966,
1971, 1976, 1992 American Bible Society.

Printed and bound in China, October 2014, LH06

NICK BUTTERWORTH AND MICK INKPEN

THE HOUSE ON THE ROCK

Here is a man.

He is looking for a place to build a house.

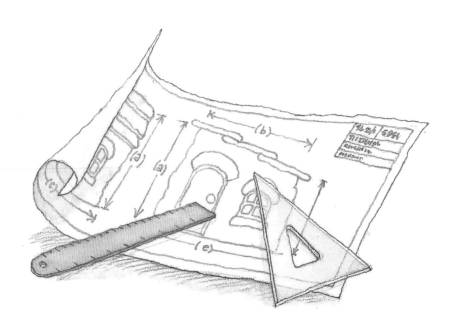

He climbs to the top of a big grey rock.

Ah! Here is a good place.

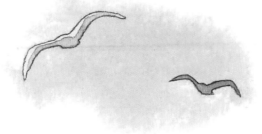

The man begins to build
his house.

It is hard work.

He puffs and pants.

He puffs and pants and grunts and groans all day, until the work is done.

'Just in time,' he says. 'It looks like rain.'

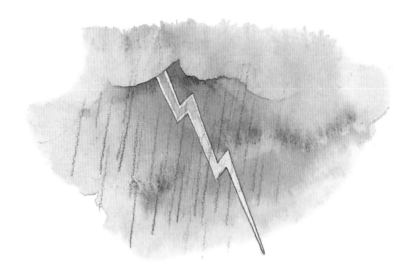

The rain pours down.

The lightning flashes.

The thunder booms.

The water washes round the house and splashes at the rock.

The rock stays firm.

The man was wise to choose
the rock.

Here is another man. He wants a house.

'I want it now. I want it quick. This place will do,' he says.

He builds his house down on the sand.

'This won't take long,' he says, and whistles as he works.

His house is done.

He goes inside and shuts the door.

A raindrop drips onto his nose.
Oh dear!

The rain pours down.

The lightning flashes.

The thunder booms.

The water rushes through the house and splashes at his knees!

The sand is washed away.

His house falls flat.

The silly man was wrong to build on sand.

Jesus says, 'I am like the
wise man's rock. If you trust me,
I will never let you down.'

Jesus said, 'So then, anyone who hears these words of mine and obeys them is like a wise man who built his house on rock. The rain poured down, the rivers overflowed, and the wind blew hard against that house. But it did not fall, because it was built on rock.

'But anyone who hears these words of mine and does not obey them is like a foolish man who built his house on sand. The rain poured down, the rivers overflowed, the wind blew hard against that house, and it fell. And what a terrible fall that was!'

Matthew 7:24–27 and Luke 6:47–49

Other titles from **Candle Books** *by*
Nick Butterworth and Mick Inkpen

The House On The Rock
The Lost Sheep
The Precious Pearl
The Good Stranger
The Two Sons
The Rich Farmer
The Ten Silver Coins
The Little Gate

Stories Jesus Told
Animal Tales
Stories Jesus Told Colouring Book